W9-ATR-728

FREDERICK COUNTY PUBLIC LIBRARIES

ORIGAMI
Folding Frenzy

Boats, Fish, Cranes, and More!

by Christopher Harbo

CAPSTONE PRESS

a capstone imprint

Edge Books are published by Capstone Press,
1710 Roe Crest Drive, North Mankato, Minnesota 56003
www.capstonepub.com

Copyright © 2015 by Capstone Press, a Capstone imprint. All rights reserved. No part of
this publication may be reproduced in whole or in part, or stored in a retrieval system, or
transmitted in any form or by any means, electronic, mechanical, photocopying, recording,
or otherwise, without written permission of the publisher.

Library of Congress Cataloging-in-Publication Data
Harbo, Christopher L., author.
  Origami folding frenzy : boats, fish, cranes, and more! / by Christopher Harbo.
     pages cm.—(Edge books. Origami paperpalooza)
  Summary: "Provides instructions and photo-illustrated step diagrams for folding a variety
of traditional and original origami models"—Provided by publisher.
  Audience: Ages 8-14.
  Audience: Grades 4 to 6.
  Includes bibliographical references.
  ISBN 978-1-4914-2021-8 (library binding)
  ISBN 978-1-4914-2192-5 (eBook PDF)
1. Origami—Juvenile literature. 2. Handicraft—Juvenile literature. I. Title.
  TT872.5.H375 2015
  736.982—dc23   2014027875

Editorial Credits
Sarah Bennett, designer; Kathy McColley, layout artist; Katy LaVigne, production specialist;
Marcy Morin, scheduler

Photo Credits
All photographs done by Capstone Studio: Karon Dubke

Design Elements: Shutterstock: naihei

Printed in Canada.
102014   008478FRS15

Table of Contents

Fantastic Folding Fun 4

Materials 5

Folding Symbols 5

Terms and Techniques 6

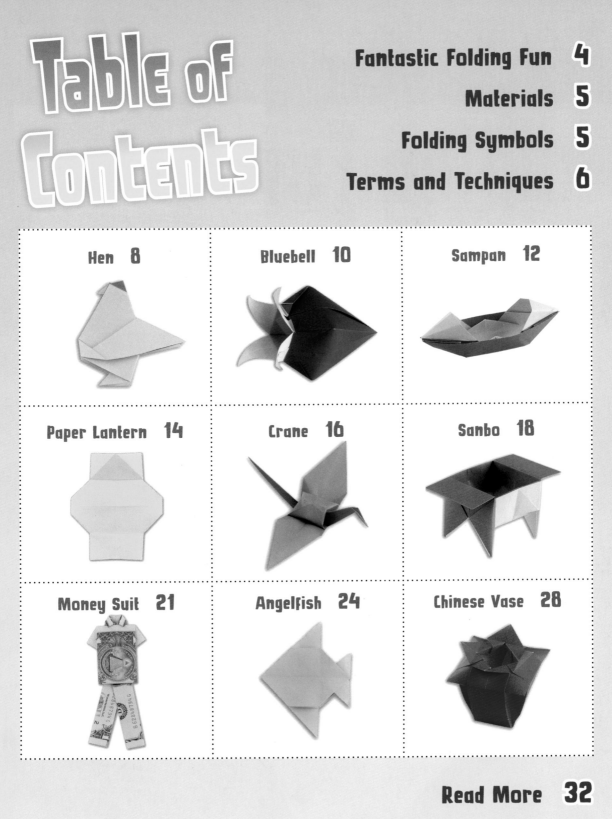

Hen 8

Bluebell 10

Sampan 12

Paper Lantern 14

Crane 16

Sanbo 18

Money Suit 21

Angelfish 24

Chinese Vase 28

Read More 32

Internet Sites 32

About the Author 32

Fantastic Folding Fun

Get ready for a paper-folding frenzy! This collection of traditional and original origami models is loaded with surprises. Impress your friends with paper boats that float. Fold money into miniature shirts and pants. Create a Chinese vase that pops up into a 3-D masterpiece. From cranes to bluebells to paper lanterns, your fingers will fold flat pieces of paper into amazing shapes. What are you waiting for? Grab some paper and let's start folding. An origami adventure awaits!

Materials

Origami is an affordable hobby because it doesn't require many materials to get started. In fact, you'll only need a square sheet of paper for most of the models in this book. A few models may require some extra materials, but you can easily find most of these items around the house:

Paper: While you can fold with just about any paper, authentic origami paper often works best. It is perfectly square, easy to fold, and has a crispness that holds its creases well. You'll find packets of origami paper with many fun colors, patterns, and sizes at most craft stores.

Scissors: Sometimes a model needs a snip here or there to pull off a key detail. You won't need it often, but keep a pair of scissors handy.

Ruler: Some models use measurements to complete. A ruler will help you measure.

Paper Trimmer: A good quality paper trimmer will come in handy when you want to cut paper to a custom size. Rotary blade paper trimmers are a good choice for precise, clean cutting. A variety of paper trimmers can be found at any craft store.

Pencil: Use a pencil when you need to mark a spot with the ruler.

Craft Supplies: Markers and other craft supplies will help you decorate your finished models.

Folding Symbols

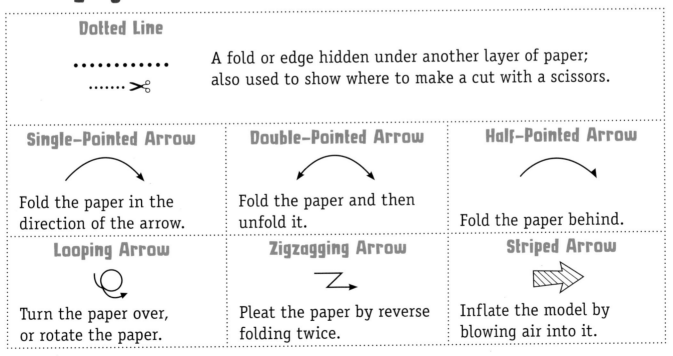

Dotted Line · · · · · · · · · · · · · · · · · ✂	A fold or edge hidden under another layer of paper; also used to show where to make a cut with a scissors.

Single-Pointed Arrow	**Double-Pointed Arrow**	**Half-Pointed Arrow**
Fold the paper in the direction of the arrow.	Fold the paper and then unfold it.	Fold the paper behind.
Looping Arrow	**Zigzagging Arrow**	**Striped Arrow**
Turn the paper over, or rotate the paper.	Pleat the paper by reverse folding twice.	Inflate the model by blowing air into it.

Terms and Techniques

Folding paper is easier when you understand basic origami folding terms and techniques. Practice the folds below before trying the models in this book. Bookmark these pages so you can refer back to them if you get stuck on a tricky step.

Valley folds are represented by a dashed line. One side of the paper is folded against the other like a book.

Mountain folds are represented by a dashed and dotted line. The paper is folded sharply behind the model.

Squash folds are formed by lifting one edge of a pocket. The pocket gets folded again so the spine gets flattened. The existing fold lines become new edges.

Inside reverse folds are made by opening a pocket slightly. Then you fold the model inside itself along the fold lines or existing creases.

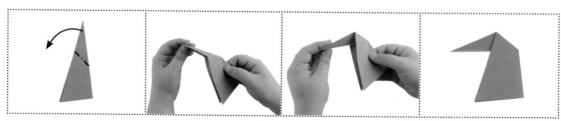

Outside reverse folds are made by opening a pocket slightly. Then you fold the model outside itself along the fold lines or existing creases.

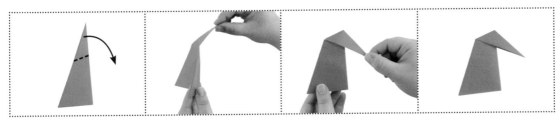

Rabbit ear folds are formed by bringing two edges of a point together using existing fold lines. The new point is folded to one side.

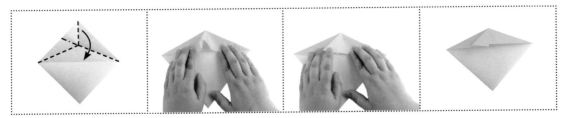

Petal folds are made by pulling a point upward and allowing its sides to come together as the paper flattens.

Pleat folds are made by using both a mountain fold and a valley fold.

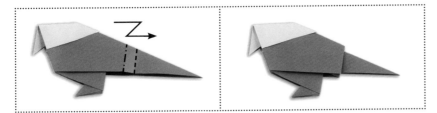

Mark folds are light folds used to make reference creases for a later step. Ideally a mark fold will not be seen in the finished model.

Hen ◆ Traditional

Here's a rare origami model that uses the white side of the paper for its main color. This hen only needs a flash of red to proudly strut her stuff.

Tip: Look for origami paper with red on one side and brown, black, or gray on the other. Then you can fold a flock of hens in a variety of colors.

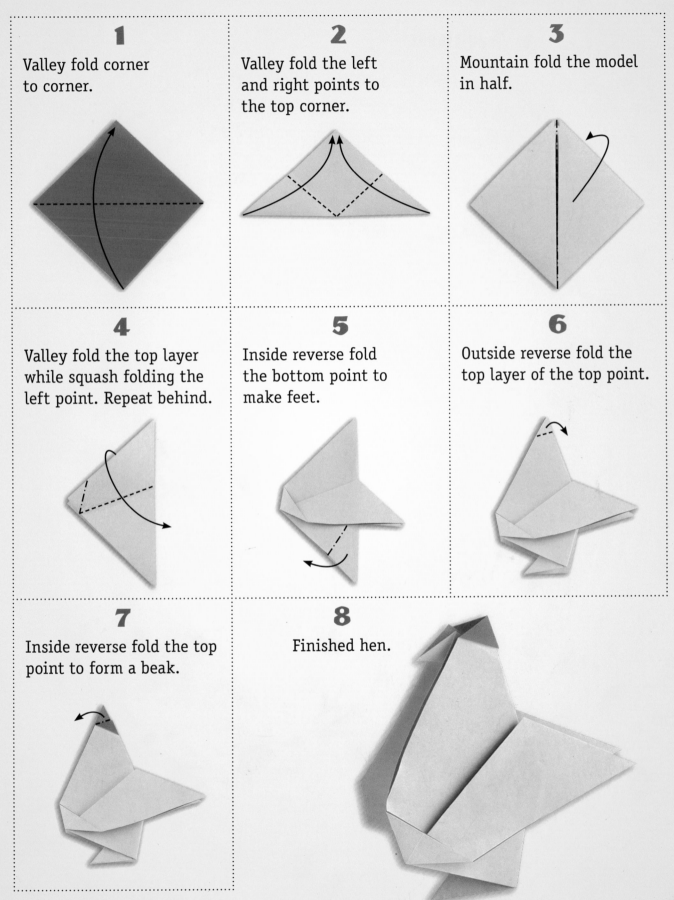

1

Valley fold corner to corner.

2

Valley fold the left and right points to the top corner.

3

Mountain fold the model in half.

4

Valley fold the top layer while squash folding the left point. Repeat behind.

5

Inside reverse fold the bottom point to make feet.

6

Outside reverse fold the top layer of the top point.

7

Inside reverse fold the top point to form a beak.

8

Finished hen.

Bluebell ◆ Traditional

Bluebells have weak stems that droop under the weight of their beautiful flowers. Fold a bouquet of these bell-shaped blossoms to brighten someone's day.

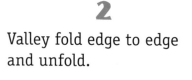

1

Valley fold corner to corner in both directions and unfold.

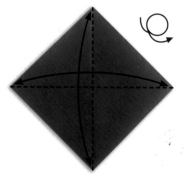

2

Valley fold edge to edge and unfold.

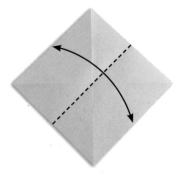

3

Valley fold edge to edge.

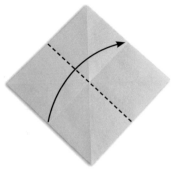

4

Squash fold.

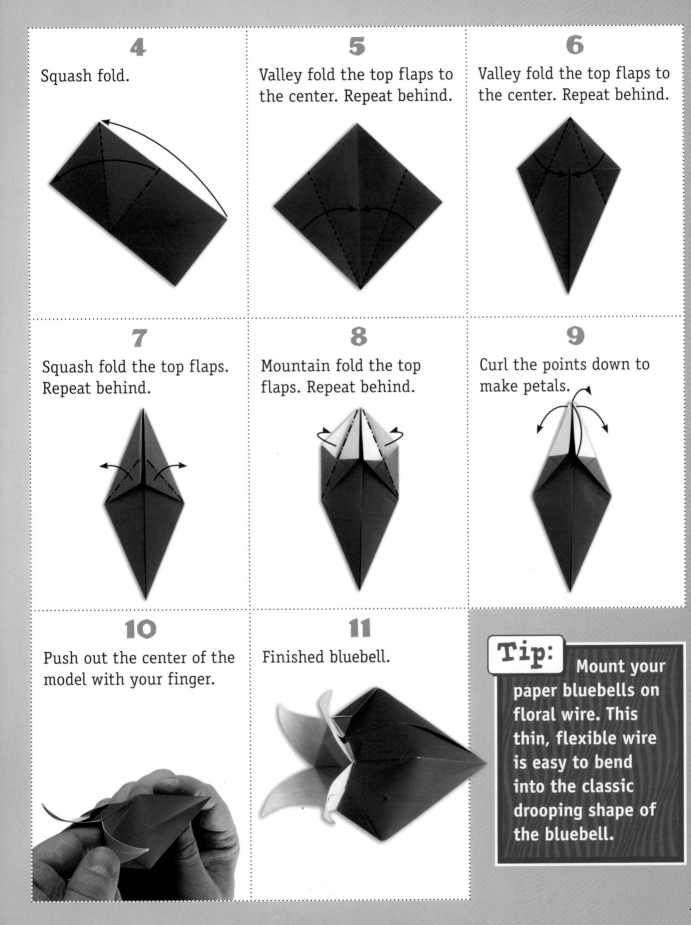

5

Valley fold the top flaps to the center. Repeat behind.

6

Valley fold the top flaps to the center. Repeat behind.

7

Squash fold the top flaps. Repeat behind.

8

Mountain fold the top flaps. Repeat behind.

9

Curl the points down to make petals.

10

Push out the center of the model with your finger.

11

Finished bluebell.

Tip:

Mount your paper bluebells on floral wire. This thin, flexible wire is easy to bend into the classic drooping shape of the bluebell.

Sampan ◆ Traditional

A sampan is a traditional flat-bottomed Chinese boat. To make this clever model, you'll actually turn the paper inside out. It sounds impossible—but it's not!

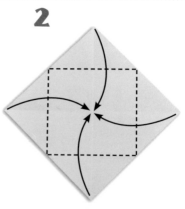

Tip: This boat really floats! To help it float even longer, color the bottom with a crayon to give it a protective layer of wax.

1

Valley fold corner to corner in both directions and unfold.

2

Valley fold all four corners to the center.

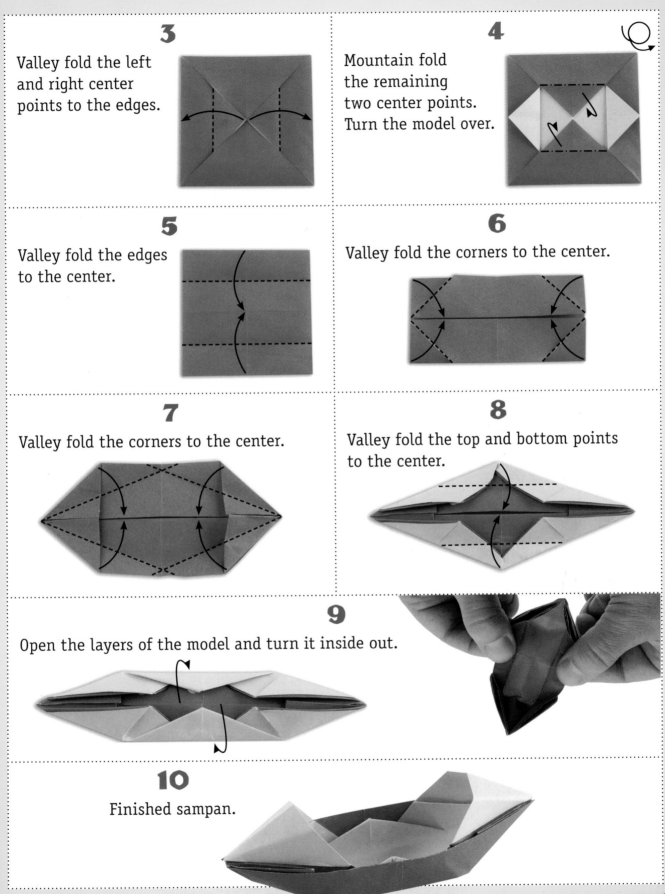

3

Valley fold the left and right center points to the edges.

4

Mountain fold the remaining two center points. Turn the model over.

5

Valley fold the edges to the center.

6

Valley fold the corners to the center.

7

Valley fold the corners to the center.

8

Valley fold the top and bottom points to the center.

9

Open the layers of the model and turn it inside out.

10

Finished sampan.

Paper Lantern ◆ Traditional

In Japan and China, paper lanterns often light up celebrations and festivals. They are also hung outside businesses to attract customers.

Tip:
Add several accordion folds to the middle of the model to give your lantern an even more life-like look.

1
Valley fold edge to edge in both directions and unfold.

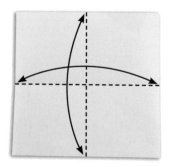

2
Valley fold the edges to the center.

3
Valley fold the corners to the center.

4

Turn the model over.

5

Valley fold the points to the center.

6

Turn the model over.

7

Valley fold the corners about ⅔ of the way to the center. Make the folds as equal as possible.

8

Turn the model over.

9

Valley fold the points up as far as they will go.

10

Pull out the paper hidden behind the points. Use existing creases to fold the extra flaps behind the model.

11

Finished paper lantern.

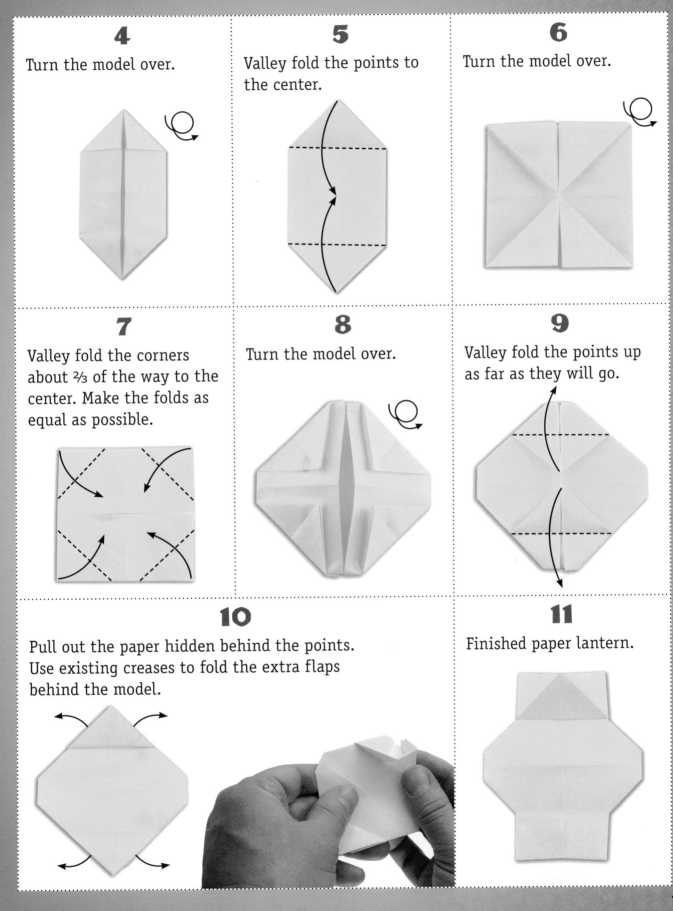

Crane ◆ Traditional

The paper crane may be the most well-known origami model in the world. Legend says folding 1,000 of these elegant birds brings good luck.

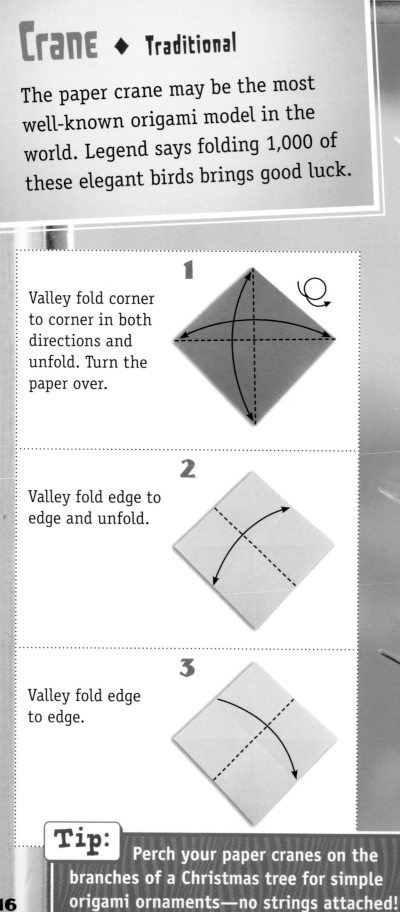

1

Valley fold corner to corner in both directions and unfold. Turn the paper over.

2

Valley fold edge to edge and unfold.

3

Valley fold edge to edge.

Tip: Perch your paper cranes on the branches of a Christmas tree for simple origami ornaments—no strings attached!

16

4
Squash fold.

5
Valley fold the top flaps to the center and unfold. Repeat behind.

6
Inside reverse fold the top flaps. Repeat behind.

7
Valley fold the top flap. Repeat behind.

8
Valley fold the top flaps to the center crease. Repeat behind.

9
Inside reverse fold the points upward.

10
Inside reverse fold the point to make the head.

11
Gently pull the wings down and apart.

12
Finished crane.

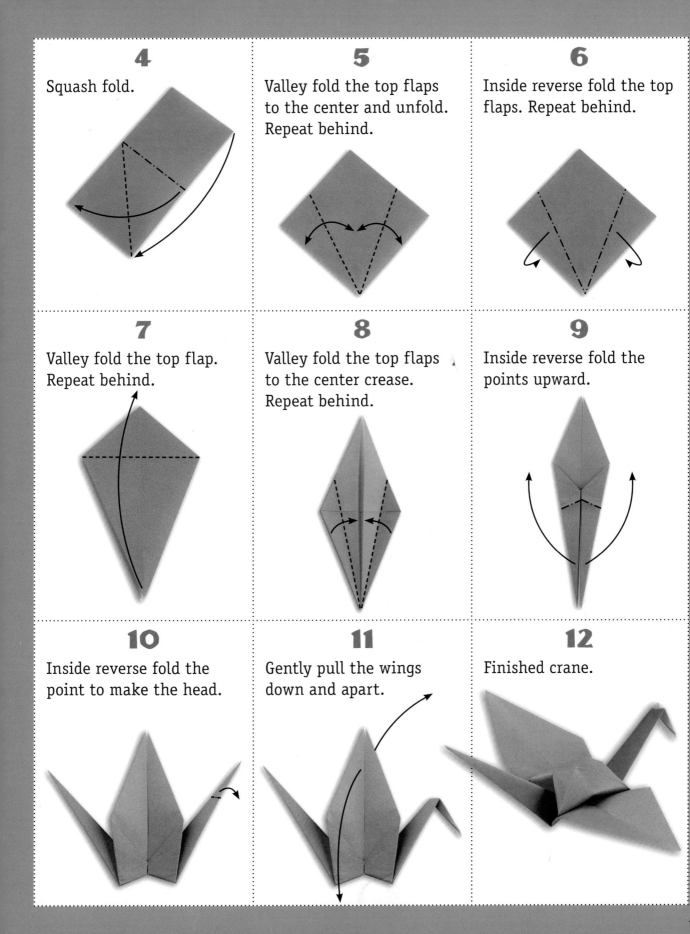

Sanbo ◆ Traditional

A sanbo is a raised serving or offering tray from Japan. This model's four legs take container origami to a whole new level.

Tip: This model shows both sides of the paper. Try folding it with a double-sided paper that has bright colors on both sides.

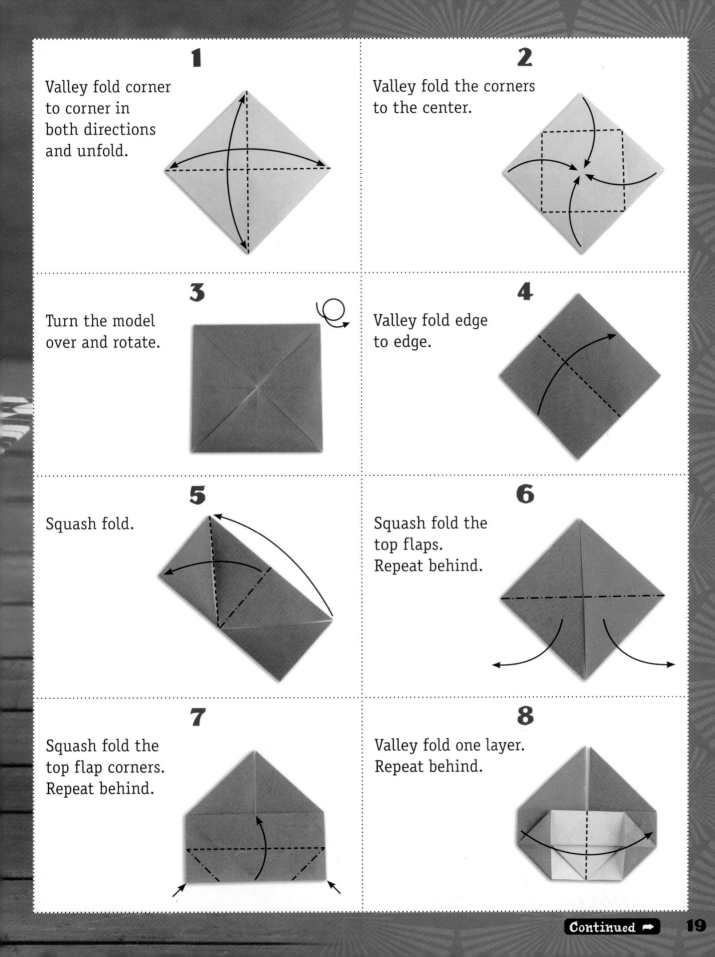

1

Valley fold corner to corner in both directions and unfold.

2

Valley fold the corners to the center.

3

Turn the model over and rotate.

4

Valley fold edge to edge.

5

Squash fold.

6

Squash fold the top flaps. Repeat behind.

7

Squash fold the top flap corners. Repeat behind.

8

Valley fold one layer. Repeat behind.

Continued ➡

9

Valley fold the inside corners of the top layer. Repeat behind.

10

Valley fold the top flaps to the center. Repeat behind.

11

Valley fold the top flap to the center. Repeat behind.

12

Valley fold the top flap. Repeat behind.

13

Gently pull apart the model to make the box.

14

Finished sanbo.

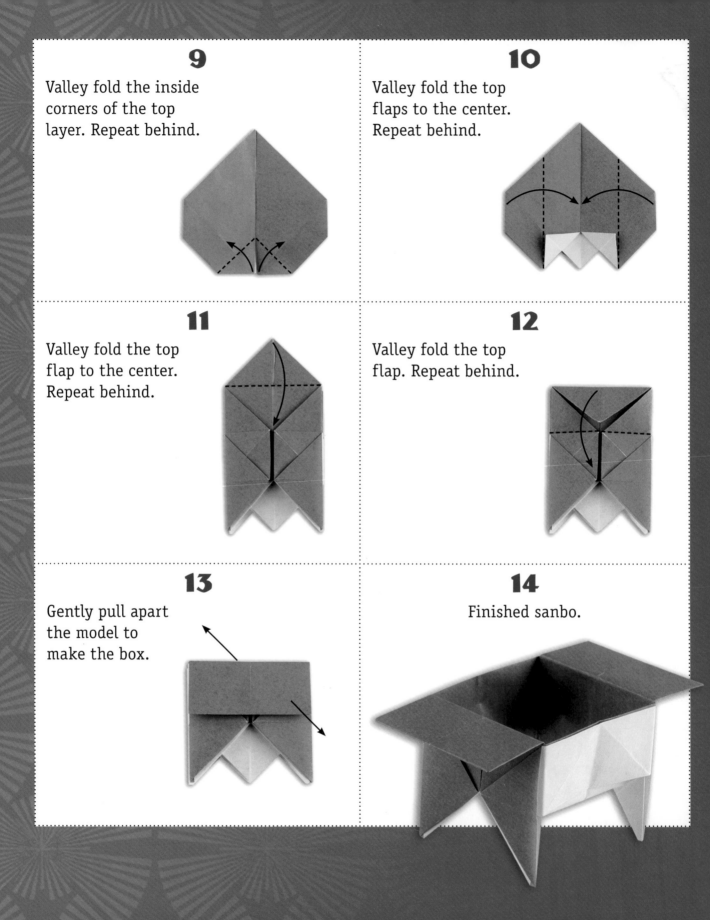

20

Money Suit ◆ Traditional

Here's a money suit that looks like a million bucks. All you need are two crisp $1 bills.

Continued ➡

Shirt

1

Valley fold edge to edge and unfold.

2

Valley fold the edges to the center and unfold. Turn the dollar over.

3

Valley fold a thin strip. Turn the dollar over.

Tip: If you're giving money as a gift, the money suit is a stylish way to insert your gift in a card.

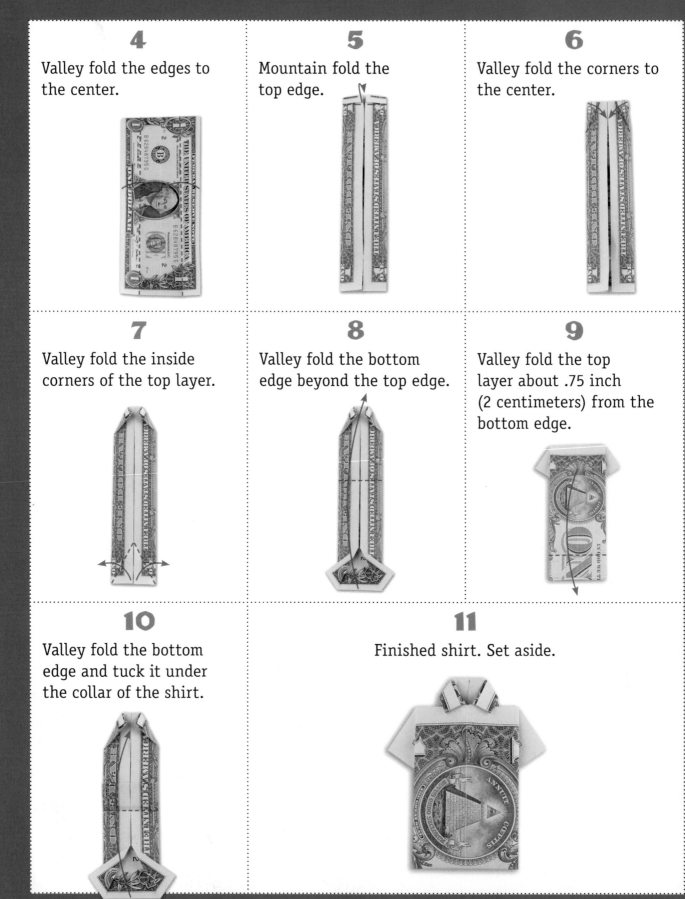

4

Valley fold the edges to the center.

5

Mountain fold the top edge.

6

Valley fold the corners to the center.

7

Valley fold the inside corners of the top layer.

8

Valley fold the bottom edge beyond the top edge.

9

Valley fold the top layer about .75 inch (2 centimeters) from the bottom edge.

10

Valley fold the bottom edge and tuck it under the collar of the shirt.

11

Finished shirt. Set aside.

12

Valley fold thin strips on each end. Turn the dollar over.

13

Valley fold edge to edge and unfold.

14

Valley fold the edges to the center.

15

Valley fold edge to edge.

16

Valley fold the model in half at a slight angle.

17

Insert pants between the bottom layers of the shirt.

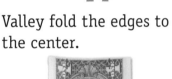

18

Finished money suit.

Tip: You don't have to fold this model out of money. Just cut regular paper to the same dimensions as a $1 bill and you're set to go.

Angelfish ◆ by Christopher Harbo

A triangle-shaped body and small tail give this angelfish its classic look. Fold a whole school of angelfish to create a beautiful underwater scene.

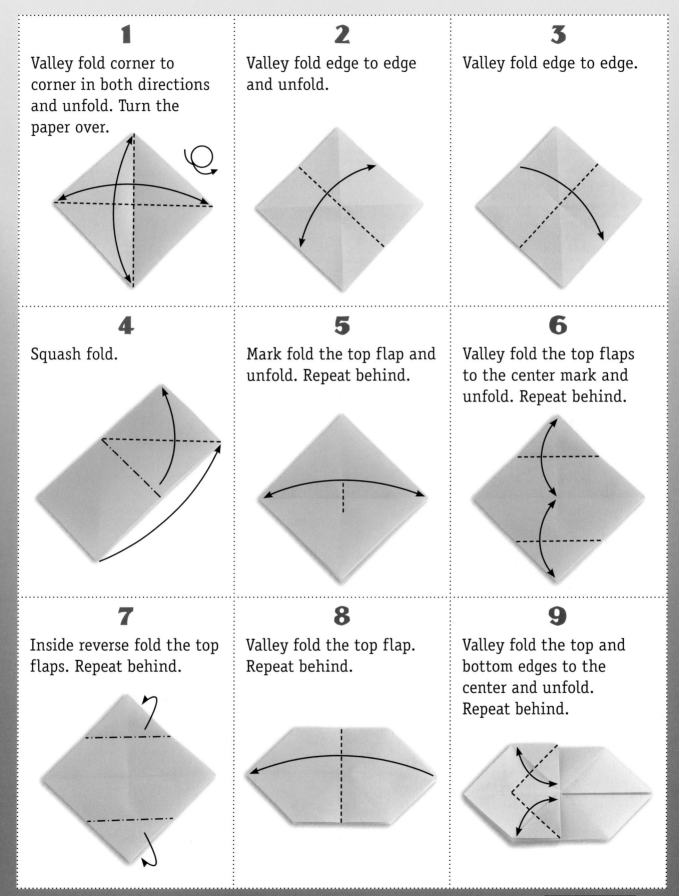

1

Valley fold corner to corner in both directions and unfold. Turn the paper over.

2

Valley fold edge to edge and unfold.

3

Valley fold edge to edge.

4

Squash fold.

5

Mark fold the top flap and unfold. Repeat behind.

6

Valley fold the top flaps to the center mark and unfold. Repeat behind.

7

Inside reverse fold the top flaps. Repeat behind.

8

Valley fold the top flap. Repeat behind.

9

Valley fold the top and bottom edges to the center and unfold. Repeat behind.

Continued ➡

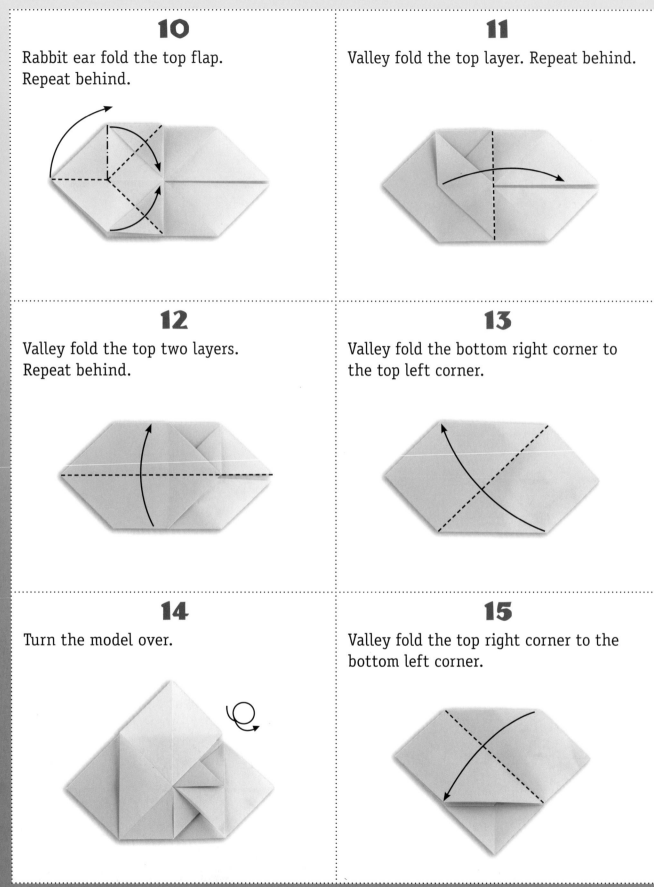

10

Rabbit ear fold the top flap. Repeat behind.

11

Valley fold the top layer. Repeat behind.

12

Valley fold the top two layers. Repeat behind.

13

Valley fold the bottom right corner to the top left corner.

14

Turn the model over.

15

Valley fold the top right corner to the bottom left corner.

16

Valley fold the top two layers.

17

Turn the model over.

18

Valley fold the top layer.

19

Valley fold the points in half. Turn the model over.

20

Finished angelfish.

Tip: Fold the angelfish in paper with color gradients. It will give the fins, tail, and body rainbow-like hues.

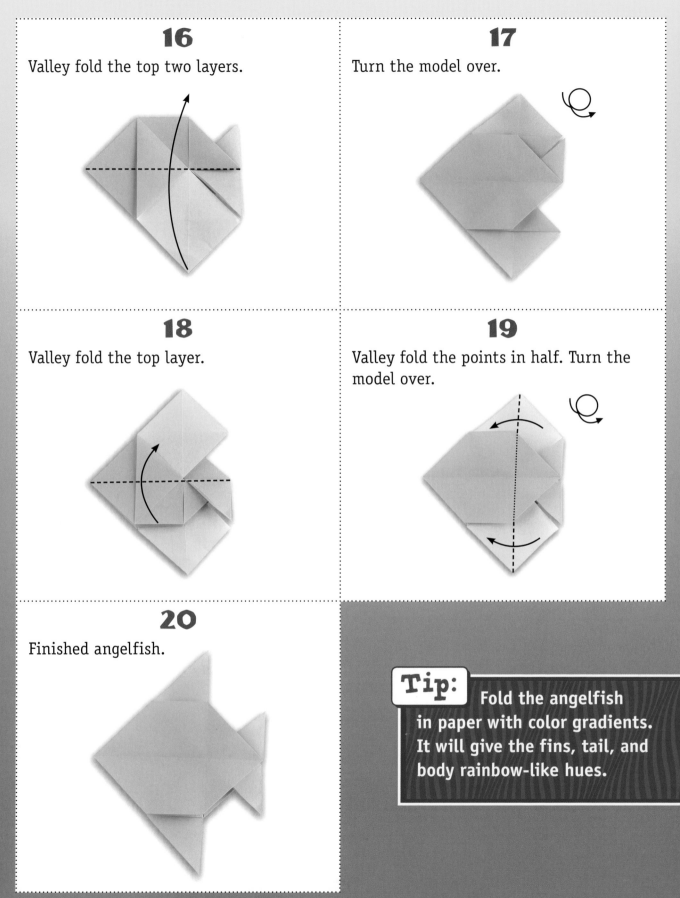

Chinese Vase ◆ Traditional

The Chinese vase turns a single square of paper into a work of art. Master this stunning model to amaze your friends and family.

Tip: Try folding the Chinese vase with a huge square of paper. Then fill it with origami flowers to make the perfect centerpiece for a table.

1

Measure and mark the square in thirds all the way around. Turn the paper over.

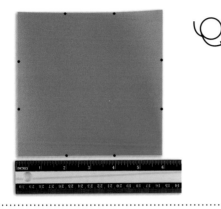

2

Valley fold at the marks made in step 1 and unfold.

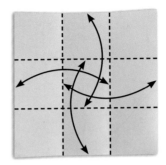

3

Valley fold halfway between all of the existing creases and unfold.

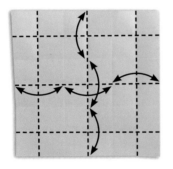

4

Valley fold halfway between creases where shown and unfold.

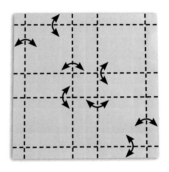

5

Pleat fold on existing creases.

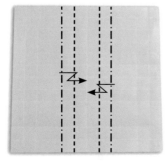

6

Pleat fold on existing creases.

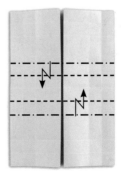

7

Turn the model over.

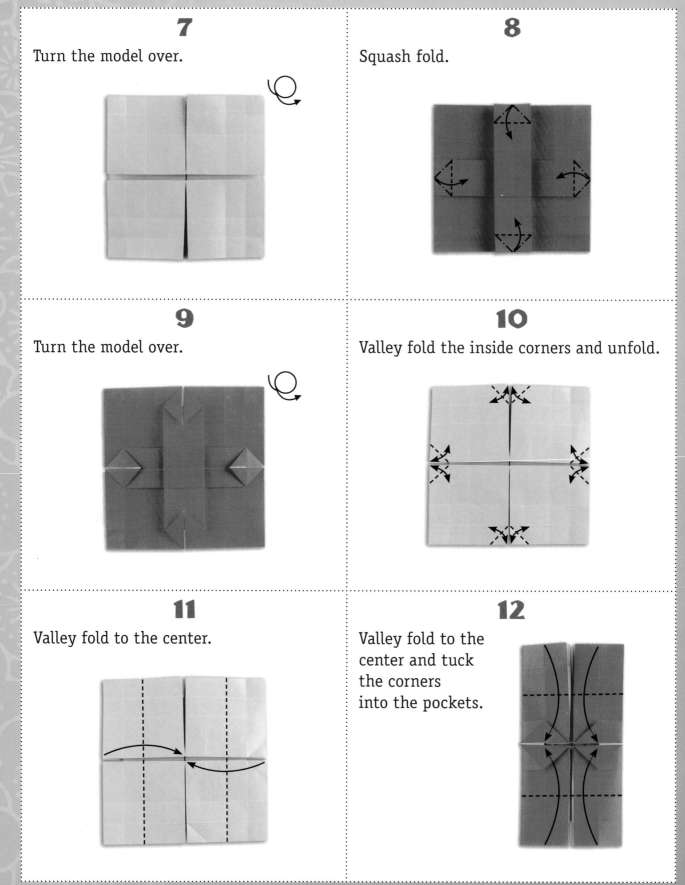

8

Squash fold.

9

Turn the model over.

10

Valley fold the inside corners and unfold.

11

Valley fold to the center.

12

Valley fold to the center and tuck the corners into the pockets.

13

Mountain fold the inside corners.

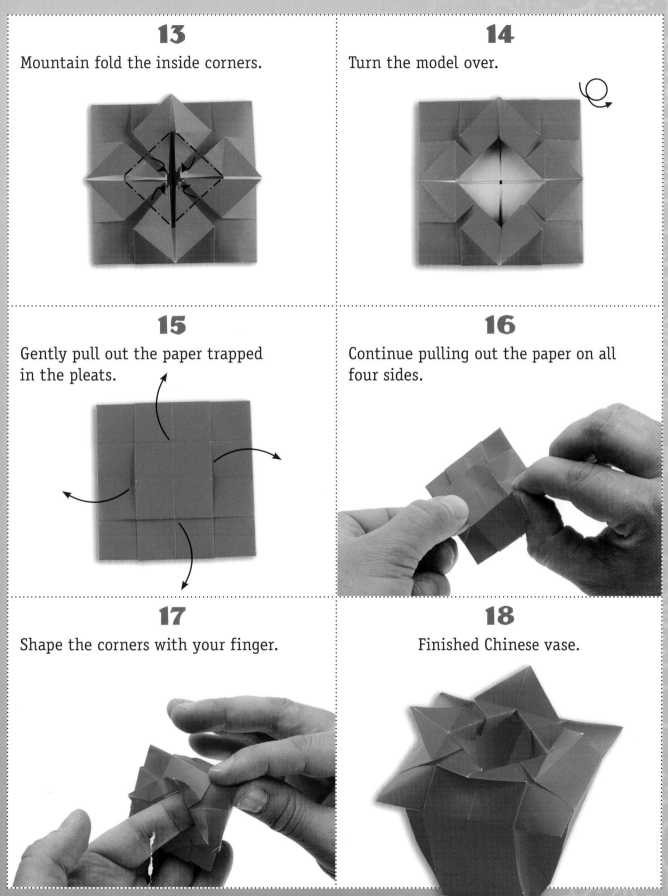

14

Turn the model over.

15

Gently pull out the paper trapped in the pleats.

16

Continue pulling out the paper on all four sides.

17

Shape the corners with your finger.

18

Finished Chinese vase.

Read More

Robinson, Nick. *Origami X: Paper Folding for Secret Agents*. North Mankato, Minn.: Capstone Press, 2013.

Miles, Lisa. *Origami Dinosaurs*. Amazing Origami. New York: Gareth Stevens Publishing, 2014.

Owen, Ruth. *Grassland Animals*. Origami Safari. New York: Windmill Books, 2015.

Internet Sites

FactHound offers a safe, fun way to find Internet sites related to this book. All of the sites on FactHound have been researched by our staff.

Here's all you do:
Visit *www.facthound.com*
Type in this code: 9781491420218

Check out projects, games and lots more at
www.capstonekids.com

About the Author

Christopher Harbo has a passion for origami. He began folding paper 10 years ago when he tried making a simple model for his nephews. With that first successful creation, he quickly became hooked on the art form. He ran to his local library and checked out every origami book he could find to increase his folding skills. Today he continues to develop his origami skills and loves the thrill of folding new creations. In addition to traditional origami and its many uses, he also enjoys folding paper airplanes and modular origami. When he's not folding paper, Christopher spends his free time reading Japanese manga and watching movies.

JUN   2015